Kildare Library & Arts Service
Seirbhís Leabharlanna & Ealaíone Chill Dara

In the interest of all library members, please return this item on or before the latest date shown below. You can renew items unless they have been requested by another member. Fines on overdue items will be charged, including the cost of postage.

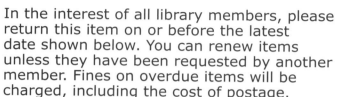

HOME SERIES
TIMELESS INTERIORS

B E T A - P L U S

CONTENTS

P. 4-5
A project carried out by 'Aksent.
Wanda settee and Valentino
chaise longue in blue mohair.
Coffee table in morado wood
and bronze.

P. 6
A Frank Tack creation: tailor-
made, hand-crafted aspect
consistent with the setting of
the dwelling.

INTRODUCTION

A timeless interior disassociates itself from the fashion phenomenon, seeing itself rather as the expression of a confident and refined taste. It invents a style that transcends the ages and appears neither dated nor bearing the imprint of time. Allergic to fashion and trends, this kind of interior design has the ability to last for years without showing its age.

Its principles? To uphold values such as the beauty of sustainable and natural materials, hand-crafted know-how, authenticity and the quality of life. What are paramount are harmony and an aestheticism based on a subtle balance.

Its secret often lies in a skilful blending to avoid the "total look". Furthermore, the pitfall of a unique decorative style generally consists in fixing and rooting an interior in a limited and rapidly obsolete temporal setting.

Without limit, from a place of timelessness comes a sense of mastery based on decoration that loves the art of subtlety.

Simple lines, a splash of fantasy, the blending of pieces that are antique, classical or exotic with designer elements or other mythical objects: these are the potential ingredients for achieving a timeless interior. Whether it has antique or contemporary connotations, its power lies in a fine association of styles, shapes and materials. Revisiting or reinterpreting a style is also an effective solution for creating a timeless atmosphere, by blurring the 'stigmata' of a particular trend. Adorned in surprising colours, 18th century mouldings are experiencing a second flush of youth.

This work presents several quite different interiors, distinguished by their simplicity and clarity, of which the common denominator is having succeeded in this difficult task: to achieve a timeless elegance.

P. 8
The warmth of the white-painted panelling for this living area of a country house. The railway train door handles are from Lerou.

P. 10-11
A creation by Alexander Cambron and Fabienne Dupont.

REMAKE OF A VERY EXCLUSIVE

DREAM VILLA

A dynamic forty-year-old, Alexander Cambron carries out three far-ranging, fully habitable residential projects every year.

Here is an example. In this villa built by Vlassak-Verhulst, everything is there to satisfy the new owners: facilities chosen for the parents' hobbies, a paradise for the children, space for sport and relaxation, a cyber-equipped office, wine cellar, home automation, music and security.

The interior decoration is the work of Fabienne Dupont.

The modern-look interior contrasts with the classical atmosphere of the house. The imposing entrance hall is open to the roof.

Note...

> A deep, muted slate-grey colour enhances antique or contemporary elements.

> The combination of tradition and modernity is the secret of timelessness. Here, a solid parquet floor takes on a contemporary look and finish: bleached appearance and extra-wide strips.

> An oversized ethnic decorative piece gives the room character on its own (pp.16-17).

The office has a wide window looking out onto the surrounding nature and gives off a feeling of tranquillity. The double-sided fireplace faces the home cinema and the second living room. The living and working areas are linked to each other but can also be quite easily separated as required, thanks to the folding doors.

P. 16-17
In this passageway between the living room and office, the 30cm wide floor is in light stained oak.

In the kitchen, Fabienne Dupont has combined dark brown oak with some splashes of bright red.

P. 20-21

The well-being area houses the fitness suite, steam room, hot tub and swimming pool, which has a removable cover which, when closed, can be used as a reception area. The huge sliding windows that look out onto the sunny terrace provide a wonderful shaft of light.

Note...

> In the kitchen, a bright red gloss-painted cupboard contrasts with the dark, matt oak and personalises the room. This original touch brightens up a contemporary atmosphere that was initially somewhat sober.

> Open or closed kitchen? A modular space that can be changed at will thanks to a wide sliding partition door.

The long open corridor that leads to the sleeping area affords a view over the entrance hall.

Decoration idea

> Make the same choices for the walk-through areas and the landing:
- the use of a dark, matt colour achieves both a timeless atmosphere and provides character and mystery;
- choosing furniture with simple lines together with natural materials is a guaranteed combination for long-lasting interior design.

The master bedroom in black and white with double-sided fireplace between the dressing area and the bedroom itself. All the bedrooms look out onto the back garden.

The master bedroom en-suite dressing area in black is made out of oak veneer with a double-sided gas fire.
The natural stone bathroom in matching tones of beige includes light side walls in white onyx both at the back of the bath and in the shower.

WARM WELL-BEING

In this feature, Mi Casa, builder of houses in solid oak, shows one of its most recent creations: an example of a very stylish classical house, the design of which focuses on the quality of life provided, the appeal and conviviality of the environment.

Houses in solid oak are pleasing and timeless buildings that naturally provide a feeling of warmth and well-being.

Decoration idea

> Absolute white: the purity associated with wood creates a timeless atmosphere focussed on comfort and tranquillity.

The swallowtail method of assembling these houses prevents beams from being crossed. As a result, the interior walls are not interrupted and the insulation of cavities in the outside walls is contiguous.

Note...

> Respect for picturesque architecture: the beamed ceilings are not hidden by a false ceiling but are on the contrary enhanced.

> Curtains, carpets and fabrics: the choice of matching materials respects the simplicity of the whole area.

> The choice of a colour tonic – bright orange – is used sparingly to liven up the interior design.

The inside walls are made from solid wood beams in redwood from northern Scandinavia. The outside walls are covered with facing bricks or cedar wood.

Great architectural freedom, dry construction and fast implementation are the major benefits of this type of house.

Decoration idea

> Purity and simplicity are always the key words in this dwelling. White walls, white curtains, spotlights on the ceiling rather than suspended lights so as not to obstruct the view towards the huge bay windows and the exterior.

The architecture and decoration are perfectly in keeping with the client's philosophy and personal wishes. The northern redwood, used throughout the house, radiates natural warmth and cosy charm.

Due to their structure and appearance, the wooden walls require little decoration. They are not bare, yet give a feeling of being finished. Moreover, they are acoustically pleasing: the occupant immediately experiences a feeling of warmth and well-being.

A MODERN HISTORIC FARM

Cretenburg Farm is a listed monument that dates from the 18th century (1771). Its restoration was vital to prevent it from collapsing.

Work on the interior of the farm was undertaken entirely by pas-partoe interieur. The architect K. Beeck, a specialist in the restoration of old buildings, coordinated the external work.

Pas-partoe made it such that the building was open and light, sober in appearance but constructed from solid and natural materials.

The restoration took two years. Certain sections were carefully taken down before being meticulously rebuilt, notably some aspects of the walls, frameworks, floors and roof. When the visible traces of somewhere rustic unashamedly rub shoulders with design, it makes for a quality renovation of a farm with character.

A settee supplied by pas-partoe. The red chair is a creation of Eames, LCW. The living room table was designed by Piet Boon.

Note...

> The timeless character of the property stems from the old architectural features of the building; whilst having been preserved, these have been reinterpreted in the image of this beamed ceiling painted in a sparkling and contemporary white, together with the designer furniture and a very modern black stained floor. A subtle blending of opposites.

> The very 'designer' red chairs enliven the whole decor.

In the kitchen, the sanded oak is in harmony with the mellowed blue stone. The kitchen appliances are hidden by a large sliding door. The table was made to measure.

Decoration idea

> The organic shape of Eero Saarinen's "Tulip" chairs contrast with the linear design of the made-to-measure kitchen and table.

The parents' bedroom with Orizzonti bed. Lamp in monastic simplicity from pas-partoe. The old painted beam contrasts superbly with the modernity of the neon lighting on the wardrobes.

In the barn, the old framework is still visible and stands imposingly, like a sculpture.

Shower in marble mosaic with fittings by Vola.

Decoration idea

> The indirect lighting behind the mirrors compensates for the lack of natural light and diffuses a soft and pleasing glow.

A PRESENT DAY COUNTRY HOUSE

This timeless country house was designed entirely by the architect Annik Dierckx. It is a composite design that easily adapts to various stages in life: from the young working family to the retired, less able-bodied couple.

The exterior as well as the interior architecture has been cared for down to the finest detail, such that all aspects are in harmony with each other. The result is a serene, harmonious and balanced whole that gives off a feeling of calm and serenity.

Throughout this house, the combination of classical elements coupled with contemporary aesthetics is to be found.

Starting from the entrance hall, in line with the front door, the living area is accessible through a double oak door. Upon entering, the straight-line axis beginning at the front door extends to the living room and fireplace. Fire is an important and recurrent theme in the living rooms of this house.

The living room leads naturally into the dining room and TV room. The latter is fitted with a gas fireplace. The dining room table affords a view towards the fireplace in the TV room, since these rooms extend from one into the other. The large sliding doors hidden in oak cupboards can, if so desired, separate the TV area from the living room and dining room.

Decoration idea

> Two elegant chandeliers, a rustic table and a contemporary triptych placed directly on the floor provide a setting and a successful blend of genres for a personal decor.

The dressing room leads to the parents' bedroom. Leading out of the dressing room are the doors to the main bathroom and the library. From the bed, you can access the bathroom through a sliding door.

The furniture in the guest bedroom is in wenge. This tropical wood imbues this room, as well as the adjoining bathroom, with natural warmth.

The main bathroom is fully accessible by wheelchair, as are the other rooms in the house. Once again, dark stained oak has been used for fitting out the bath and washbasin cupboards. The sand-coloured, shaped ceramic tiles are slip resistant.

AUTHENTIC AND TIMELESS

D oran for country cooking designs and creates interiors with a personalised stamp for new build and renovation projects.

A team of interior architects and colour advisers undertake the creation of complete tailor-made interiors.

Around the kitchen, the focal point of the house, Doran for country cooking builds an interior from A to Z in an uncluttered or country style.

Decoration idea

> A sheen effect, admittedly classical for an old dwelling but combined with an unexpectedly bold colour – slate-grey/blue – has the effect of modernising the whole area.

An authentic tap adorns the sink. Doran solid wood furniture.

The laundry room is in a country style, with its painted solid oak furniture topped with Belgian blue stone. The floor tiles from the Doran "fleur de lys" collection are in natural stone.

P. 59-63
The kitchen is fitted with a cast-iron Nobel cooker and solid oak furniture enhanced with moulded Belgian blue stone.
The handmade wall tiles are from the Doran collection.

The bathroom is fitted with an open shower. Solid pine furniture. Solid oak door from the Doran collection. The triptych mirror is encased in a shaped oak frame.

The painted MDF dressing table has a matching oak shelf.

The oak floorboards are from the Doran collection. Pine wall furniture, oak shelf with an integrated linen storage unit.

LUXURY AND SOBRIETY

FOR A TIMELESS APARTMENT

This luxury apartment was designed by the firm Costermans, in collaboration with Studio Het Arsenaal owned by Jan des Bouvrie.

The classical Parisian architectural facade maintains its pure design and brings together certain structural lines: high ceilings, impressive spaces and great light.

Natural colours, materials and fabrics were chosen, broken up by touches of lilac and mauve.

Works of art from the Het Arsenaal collection provide the finishing touches.

Decoration idea

> Look out for a stunning entrance hall. The oversized and intimidating mirror in the entrance hall creates a surprising optical effect.

> The classically inspired bench covered in padded lilac velvet provides a priceless touch as well as puts a finishing touch to the decor.

In front of the simple living room fireplace, a cosy lounge.
Behind the armchairs, a wall bookcase with pure lines.

P. 70-71
The frivolous pastel-coloured cushions contribute a warm and playful touch to the lounge area. The lamps are from Verner Panton.

Note...

> In this kitchen/dining area, only two elements disturb the contemporary setting: a huge rustic wooden table is modernised with a varnished finish for greater sophistication and is in pleasing contrast with a priceless chandelier.

The kitchen adjoining the dining room has a wooden table in recycled pallet wood. Cupboards with hidden handles in ultra-shiny gloss and thick Corian worktop.

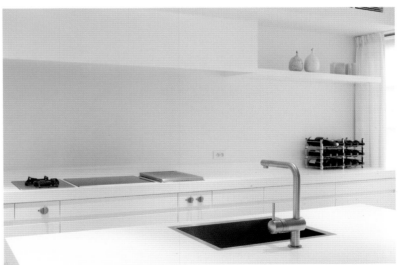

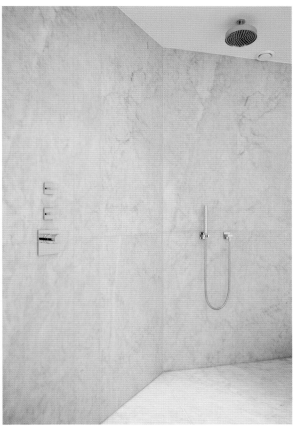

Harmonious blend of Carrara marble and oak boards. The whole apartment floor is covered with oak flooring, which gives an impression of space and continuity.

A romantic bedroom with a compact little desk.

A SPLIT-LEVEL APARTMENT

OF GENEROUS PROPORTIONS

This split-level penthouse apartment is exceptional in many respects: it is a luxury apartment with the appearance and surface area of a vast landscape, affording a unique view over the sea.

All the finishes are top-of-the-range: the design and creation of the ground floor were entrusted to Obumex, who also carried out the work on the upper floors, based on a project by the interior architect Philip Simoen.

Note...

> The choice of mixed and timeless but nonetheless warm colours distinguishes this interior and provides a chic overall effect.

In the entrance hall, flooring in Cotto d'Este Buxy flammé. Sahco Hesslein curtains.

P. 80-83
Living room with view over the sea. JNL Collection furniture. Sahco Hesslein fabrics and curtains.

P. 84-87
The fireplace and TV area were designed and created by Obumex.
JNL armchairs; Sahco Hesslein fabrics.
The living room corner takes on a more distinctive style with ethnic touches that apply in particular to the low tables. The wood panelling endows the room with refined luxury.

JNL furniture was also selected for the dining room.

Decoration idea

> Juxtapose various floorings to define and suggest specific areas, such as here with textured tiling for the dining room separating the TV room with parquet flooring.

The dressing room adjoining the master bedroom was designed and created by Obumex.
JNL bed, Sahco Hesslein fabrics.

Hall and staircase providing access to the guest bedrooms. Stéphane Davidts lighting.

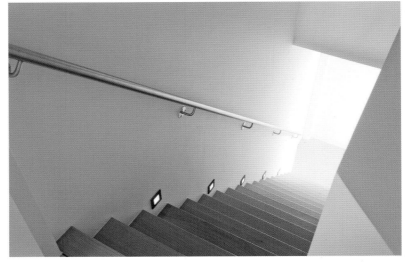

A guest bedroom, decorated with Sahco Hesslein fabrics.

MINIMALISM

IN AN INTIMATE SETTING

T he renowned interior architect, Francis Luypaert, favours minimalist, simple designs within warm and intimate settings.

This feature presents one of his recent projects. Celebration of space and light are the hallmarks of this interior.

The renovation of this entrance hall in a minimalist contemporary style was developed using made-to-measure furniture in conjunction with laminated, dark-stained oak reproducing the colours of mural finishes. Non-grained, flame finish Pietra Piasentina flooring was selected. Window frame with hidden outline.

Note...

> The difference is in the detail, such as the light points on the stair risers, the very convenient staircase with shallow, wide steps and the carefully thought out lighting with neon lights integrated into the false ceiling.

> Attention to the entrance is an indication of the style of the rest of the dwelling. Here, the suspended side table seems to be levitating and extends from the other side of the wall, an original concept.

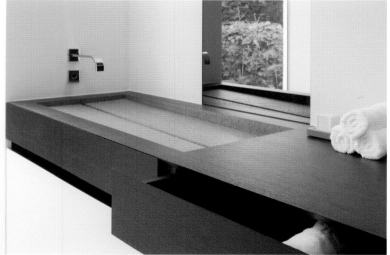

The hallway leading to the bedrooms with built-in cupboards, painted entirely in the same matt chalk colour as the wall. This colour is linked to the solid oak floor, which was chosen in naturally grey, non-grained straight fibres with an oil varnish. The méridienne sofa is covered in a cotton fabric.

The ultra shiny white-lacquered MDF table - created by Francis Luypaert - is framed by 1970s retro-styled chairs, restored using matt white leather. Modular lighting (Bolster chrome) and white half-pipe. A ceramic sculpture by Lieven Demunter and a Francis Luypaert canvas. On the floor, a zebra skin.

Decoration idea

> Enhance an omnipresent and immaculate white by using multiple materials and textures: gloss, leather, matt painting, etc.

In the children's bathroom, greyish-beige colours are preferred. Bathroom furniture and cupboards are in MDF with hand-painted joints. The shower and wall behind the washbasin are tiled with Moroccan zelliges.
Surface in natural polished Moleanos stone. Wall lights by Stéphane Davidts.

The large, main bathroom has a bath and walk-in shower, fitted with highly functional built-in cupboards. The whole room is adorned with classical panelling. The rain shower was integrated into the ceiling with a ventilation system.
The walls of the shower are decorated in hammered marble mosaic.
The surface of the washbasin and bath is finished in polished Emperador Dark marble with classical framing.

FACELIFT

FOR A CLASSICAL MANSION

This project – giving a new look to a mansion – was entrusted to the interior architect Stephanie Laporte.

This majestic abode underwent a complete metamorphosis: the classical architectural appearance made way for a pure, minimalist and contemporary design.

In the made-to-measure living room, a dark wood living room table. Light stained oak floor and velvet curtains.

Dark wooden wall units teamed with a mirror and lacquered glass. Chandelier with crystal charms.

Decoration idea

> Inject a touch of luxury and affectation into a sober and masculine world such as here with a reflecting chandelier above a rectangular table: one style enhances another.

P. 106-107
View of the dining room from
the living room.

Decoration idea

> Table armchairs rather than ordinary chairs for greater comfort and originality.

> Maxi pendant light: an effective solution to define and enhance the dining area.

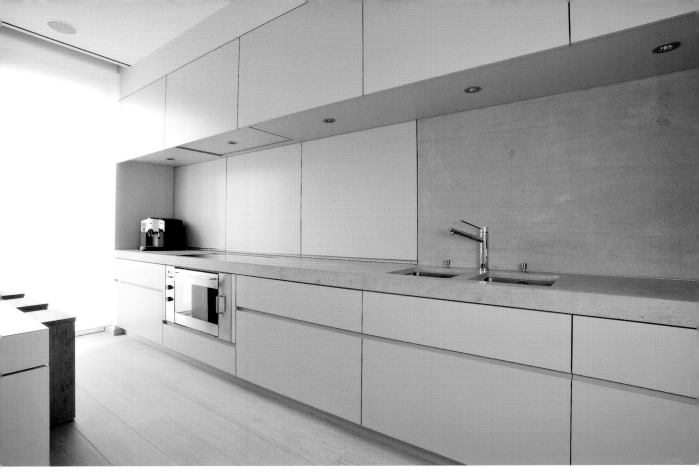

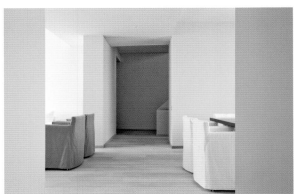

The kitchen was made to measure in matt lacquered MDF and beige natural stone. The bleached floor, omnipresent throughout the house, is harmoniously integrated in the kitchen.

SYMBIOSIS OF ELEGANCE

AND FUNCTIONALITY

B ourgondisch Kruis carries out restoration and interior decoration projects in a timeless style that combines elegance with a functional aspect.

To this end, the company has its own carpentry workshop, from which experienced professionals provide impeccable made-to-measure work using oak panels, as well as a stone-cutting workshop.

The house presented here has a revisited country feeling. In this environment, colour is used to modernise the country style.

An original Louis XIV fireplace, in Burgundy stone.

A 17th century oak floor. In the hallway, flooring in antique Burgundy flagstones laid in Roman style. The steps of the staircase are in solid Burgundy wood with a wrought iron hand rail. Solid washbasin. Panelling in antique oak boards.

Decoration idea

> In the hallway, the use of gloss paint does not undermine the feeling of the property but its grey tonality brings it up-to-date with a more modern style.

P. 112-115

This kitchen was designed and created entirely by Bourgondisch Kruis. The blue stone of the worktops, the sink, the supporting walls and the trim on the wall behind the cooker are in harmony with the antique oak plank cupboards. Flooring in antique blue stone tiles (50cm x 50cm). The blue stone framework of the barbecue was built using little terracotta tiles. Here again the grey walls add a contemporary touch.

Wrought iron banisters and folding door.

In this bathroom furnished with solid washbasins in Burgundy stone, natural Burgundy stone was also selected for the flooring. Smooth-finished rectangular tiles were used.

The bedroom is panelled using old oak boards.

P. 118-119
The cupboards next to the fireplace are made out of old oak panels.

HOME SERIES

Volume 27 : TIMELESS INTERIORS

The reports in this book are selected from the Beta-Plus collection of home-design books: www.betaplus.com
They have been compiled in a special series by Le Figaro in French language: Ma Déco.

Copyright © 2010 Beta-Plus Publishing / Le Figaro
Originally published in French language

PUBLISHER
Beta-Plus Publishing
Termuninck 3
B – 7850 Enghien
Belgium
www.betaplus.com
info@betaplus.com

TEXT
Alexandra Druesne

PHOTOGRAPHY
Jo Pauwels

DESIGN
Polydem - Nathalie Binart

TRANSLATIONS
Txt-Ibis

ISBN : 978-90-8944-081-5

Printed in China

P. 122-123
Smooth finish floor in Massangis, created by Van den Weghe (The Stonecompany).
A Filip Tack Design Office project.

P. 124-125
Home cinema fitted with a gas fireplace. Fireplace from Van den Bogaert Leon.

P. 126-127
A project by Alexander Cambron and Fabienne Dupont.